ONE DIRECTION

UNOFFICIAL

Nadia Cohen
Foreword by Mango Saul

**FLAME TREE
PUBLISHING**

Contents

ONE DIRECTION

HA

Sandwell
Metropolitan Borough Council

Please return this item to any Sandwell Library on or before the return date.

You may renew the item unless it has been reserved by another borrower.

You can renew your library items by using the 24/7 renewal hotline number - 0845 352 4949
or FREE online at opac-lib.sandwell.gov.uk

THANK YOU FOR USING YOUR LIBRARY

07 FEB

2 5 AUG 2015

Publisher and Creative Director: Nick Wells
Project Editor & Picture Research: Polly Prior
Art Director: Mike Spender
Layout Design: Jane Ashley
Digital Design and Production: Chris Herbert

Special thanks to: Laura Bulbeck, Emma Chafer, Esme Chapman, Jane Donovan,
Stephen Feather, Karen Fitzpatrick, Dawn Laker

FLAME TREE PUBLISHING
Crabtree Hall, Crabtree Lane
Fulham, London SW6 6TY
United Kingdom
www.flametreepublishing.com

Website for this book: www.flametreepop.com

First published 2013

13 15 17 16 14
1 3 5 7 9 10 8 6 4 2

© 2013 Flame Tree Publishing Ltd

A CIP record for this book is available from the British Library upon request.

ISBN 978-0-85775-864-4

Printed in China

Foreword

Simon Cowell could see One Direction coming a mile off. Five young, good-looking chaps with reasonable singing voices and charm that would make any girl fall for them. TA DA! 1D were formed, as if by magic. *The X Factor* guru knew exactly what he was creating when he brought together Zayn Malik, Niall Horan, Louis Tomlinson, Liam Payne and Harry Styles – a boy band that were going to make him a ton of cash by selling millions of records. Globally.

Having the fastest-selling album of 2011 is a mean accomplishment. Being the first UK group to ever bag a No. 1 in the US Billboard 200 is achieving the almost-impossible. Not even six-album Take That have mastered the US charts like One Direction have in just two. Actually, we need to forget Take That and any other boy band you can think of: we've not seen a pop phenomenon like One Direction since The Beatles and Beatlemania.

Some people may think that putting One Direction in the same sentence as The Beatles is complete madness, especially since the *X Factor* not-even-runners-up have only released two albums and a handful of singles. It's not madness. The band has charisma, good song writers behind them and, more importantly, Simon Cowell and his company Syco orchestrating the perfect pop machine.

If anyone thinks what One Direction have achieved so far is utterly amazing, we haven't seen anything yet. There's plenty more to come from this fresh new quintet...

Mango Saul
Editor, Sugarscape.com

New British Invasion

In September 2010, the world had never heard of Harry Styles, Niall Horan, Liam Payne, Zayn Malik and Louis Tomlinson. The five boys did not even know each other's names and yet, within just 18 months of meeting each other, the singers – who joined forces to create the global phenomenon that is One Direction – had made history.

And on 21 March 2012, they became the first-ever UK group to debut at No. 1 on the American Billboard chart with their album, *Up All Night.* Previously, the highest entry for a UK group's debut was when the Spice Girls unleashed *Spice* in 1997; they had cracked America in style.

When One Direction heard about their record-breaking moment, they were in the middle of a jam-packed promotional tour across the States, causing pandemonium to break out wherever they went, as thousands of love-struck fans turned out for a glimpse of the biggest British group since The Beatles landed, almost 50 years earlier.

'We've got a lot of big dreams. We want to have No. 1s, travel a lot, go back to America and have as much fun as possible – I don't think that's too much to ask!'

Harry Styles

Making It Happen

Before they even set foot on American soil, One Direction were already superstars, thanks to clever use of social media. Executives from their label, Columbia Records, decided to use Facebook and Twitter for their marketing campaign instead of the usual strategy of releasing a single on the radio. Taking a gamble, co-chairman Steve Barnett decided to mount a four-month, word-of-mouth campaign with the intention of building a fan base before a single was ever released or even played on the radio in America. Columbia asked fans to sign petitions and enter video competitions to win a concert in their hometown.

The gamble paid off spectacularly well and, within a few weeks, One Direction's Facebook page had 400,000 followers in the States. Their single 'What Makes You Beautiful' sold more than 131,000 copies, although it had yet to be played on the radio. In fact, radio stations were flooded with calls from fans demanding to hear their songs before the boys had even left London.

'It feels so strange when I look back to before The X Factor, when I didn't even have a passport and hadn't been outside the UK. Now all of a sudden I've been to all of these amazing places.'

Zayn Malik

The Boys Are Back In Town

Back home in the UK, there was just as much excitement about the band's success, with cameras and love-struck admirers following their every move. They may have only come third on *The X Factor* (2010), but Simon Cowell spotted their potential and the boys were immediately signed to his record label, Syco. Syco's managing director Sonny Takhar believes their runaway success is all down to the power of social media. 'It's a real moment,' he says. 'Social media has become the new radio – it's never broken an act globally like this before.' The boys have millions of 'likes' on Facebook, and although each of the boys has their own Twitter account, which they update several times a day, the band's management also employs a social media team to keep up with the relentless demand from fans responding to the boys' every word.

'People think that a boy band is air-grabs and being dressed in all one colour. We're boys in a band – we're trying to do something different from what people would think is the typical kind of boy band. We're trying to do different kinds of music and we're just trying to be ourselves, not squeaky clean.'

Niall Horan

Getting Together

The boys all auditioned as individual contestants on the seventh series of
ITV1's talent show *The X Factor* in 2010 and that was the moment when
everything in their lives was changed for ever. That year, Simon Cowell was
the mentor for the groups and declared himself 'genuinely very excited' about
One Direction, who quickly became his best hope of winning the competition.
Their performances provoked such loud screams from the studio audience
that the judges' comments could hardly be heard. Amid all the hysteria, Simon
confidently predicted his group were going to win: 'They get on well and they
have steel in their eyes, and that's what I look for in my artists,' he noted.
'I think they'll go far.'

*'We played a lot of gigs once the series
finished and it was all new for me – I'd
never even been to a nightclub before. I
lived a very quiet, boring and sheltered life
before the band, so absolutely everything
that happened was a learning curve.'*

Zayn Malik

'The best moment for me out of the whole thing was when we were told we were going to be put in a band together, but I never for a moment thought that things would end up like this.'

Harry Styles

Making Waves

When *The X Factor* final was over, the boys were devastated at missing out on the top prize and were all in tears until Simon Cowell called his favourite group into his dressing room, backstage at the Fountain Studios in Wembley, and made an announcement. 'You were great on the show,' he told them. 'Sony are going to sign you up in the morning. You're going to be all right, don't worry about coming third,' he added, before giving them all a hug, but urging them to keep the news secret until after Christmas.

In January 2011, One Direction signed a £2m record contract with Simon's company Syco before heading off to LA for five days to record some early tracks in the first professional recording studio any of them had ever seen. But there was no time to complete an album, for they were contractually obliged to spend the next three months on *The X Factor* Live Tour. The UK tour, which kicked off in February at the LG Arena in Birmingham, was a triumph.

Up All Night

One Direction's debut album – *Up All Night* – was released in the UK in November 2011 and four months later in the States, featuring 13 songs that the boys co-wrote with a series of top producers who had worked with Lady Gaga, Beyoncé and Britney Spears. They began work as soon as they had finished filming *The X Factor*, once Simon Cowell had signed them to Syco Music. Being runners-up on the show proved no barrier to success and the catchy first single from the album, 'What Makes You Beautiful', sold more than 100,000 copies in its first weekend and topped the iTunes chart within 13 minutes of being released.

The fastest-selling album of the year, it debuted at No. 2 in the UK and was only kept off the top spot by Rihanna's *Talk That Talk*. It went on to top the charts in Australia, Croatia, Italy, Mexico, New Zealand and Sweden, reaching the Top 10 in a total of 20 countries. The hysteria surrounding their first release led to comparisons with Westlife and Take That, who the boys all idolize.

'Our aim with the album was to recreate the boy band sound, do something no one else is doing at the moment.'

Niall Horan

Critical Reaction

As well as the fans loving it, *Up All Night* also went down a storm with music critics, who raved about its anthemic pop songs and youthful lyrics about having fun and heartbreak. The boys were thrilled when 'What Makes You Beautiful' won the BRIT Award for Best British Single at the 2012 ceremony at London's O2 Arena.

The first three singles taken from *Up All Night* went straight into the UK Top 10 and 'What Makes You Beautiful' became the most pre-ordered single in Sony Music Entertainment history. It also topped the charts in Australia and New Zealand, the Flemish Ultratop 50 and the Canadian Hot 100.

'To be thrown together like that and have to get to know each other was a bit scary. We're all quite different as well, so we did bicker occasionally. We get on brilliantly now, though. As soon as we were honest with each other it worked, and we've ended up being really close mates.'

Liam Payne

What Makes You Beautiful

When One Direction released their debut single on 11 September 2011, it broke the pre-order sales record for Sony Music. A week later, 'What Makes You Beautiful' stormed into the UK Singles Chart at No. 1, having sold 153,965 copies – the highest first-week sales for any song that year. It would remain at No. 1 in the UK and Ireland for four weeks. Days later, One Direction announced their debut UK dates and tickets for the Up All Night Tour were sold out within minutes of being released. When the single was released in America in February 2012, it debuted on the Billboard Hot 100, going on to peak at No. 4 for two weeks.

'It was nerve-wracking, trying to find the first single, because of course we wanted it to be perfect. We all got to do a lot of co-writing, which was really important for us and we loved being involved.'

Liam Payne

All About The Boys

Within days of their first appearance on TV, each of the boys had become known for a particular feature. Niall is now 'the cute little Irish one', Zayn is 'the quiet and mysterious one', Liam is 'the sensible one', Harry is 'the charming one' and Louis is 'the funny one'.

Luckily, the lads do not seem to mind the labels but Niall is determined they should not be seen as being the same as all the other boy bands around.

'I'm 16 and I want to be a big name like Beyoncé and Justin Bieber. I've been compared to him a few times and it's not a bad comparison. I want to sell out arenas, make an album and work with some of the best artists in the world!'
Niall Horan, to X Factor judges

at his audition

Niall

Niall James Horan was born on 13 September 1993 in the small town of Mullingar, Ireland. Following his parents' divorce when he was five, Niall and his brother Greg eventually decided to live with their father Bobby when mum, Maura, remarried in 2005. Niall was a popular pupil at Colatitude Muire, a school for boys founded by the Christian Brothers. Although he did not excel academically, teachers recall that he was good at French and showed great potential.

Niall was into music from a very young age; at six years old, he started to play the recorder and took up the guitar aged 12. Before his big break, Niall was chosen as a support act for a previous *X Factor* contestant, Lloyd Daniels, when he performed in Dublin and was brimming with confidence when he himself auditioned for the show soon afterwards.

'It's amazing how word spreads about where we are. We do have to be a bit more careful because even if we just pop out to get something and people recognize us, it can go a bit crazy.'

Niall Horan

Zayn

Born on 12 January 1993, Zayn grew up with three sisters in Bradford, where he attended Tong High School. He was a bright kid and by the age of eight had a reading age of 18, as well as a talent for art and drama. He joined the school choir and was cast in productions of Grease, Arabian Nights and Bugsy Malone. Although he says he still feels like that kid from Bradford, Zayn is now recognized everywhere he goes.

The only member of the band who smokes, Zayn also has many tattoos including a Yin Yang Tai-Chi symbol on his wrist, the word 'ZAP!' on his forearm, his grandfather's name 'Walter' in Arabic on his chest, a 'born lucky' symbol on his stomach, a silver fern on his neck and an inscription across his collarbone that says 'be true to who you are' in Arabic.

'A year ago, the thought of being on stage in front of that many people would have been enough to make me physically sick, but now I go out and walk around the stage and I feel so much more confident.'

Zayn Malik

Liam

Liam James Payne gave his parents, Karen and Geoff, quite a scare when he was born three weeks early on 29 August 1993 and needed resuscitation. As a result, one of his kidneys was scarred and dysfunctional. Now one kidney does not work and so he has to be careful not to drink too much – even water – and to stay healthy.

As a child, Liam was always singing karaoke and joined the school choir when he was nine. He even won a solo, aged 13, when his choir joined with other schools to set a new world record for the number of people singing in unison.

Because of his kidney problems, Liam watches his diet carefully, particularly the amount of salt and protein he consumes, and prefers to unwind by working out in the gym. As a result, he has impressive six-pack abs to show for it and is happy to be known as the 'dad' of the group.

'It was horrible to be turned away, but if I had made the live shows I wouldn't have known what hit me – I would have been gone straight away!'

Liam Payne

Harry

1 February 1994 was the day when the world welcomed Harry Edward Styles to his family home in Holmes Chapel, Cheshire. His parents divorced when Harry was seven and they moved into the pub, run by Anne. Five years later, their mother married Robin Twist.

Ever since he was at nursery school, Harry has loved performing to an audience and has appeared in productions of Chitty Chitty Bang Bang and Barney. He was also a keen singer and, when his grandfather, Harold, gave him a karaoke machine, he learned all the words to dozens of Elvis Presley songs.

Harry became the lead singer with a local band called White Eskimo, and they won a Battle of the Bands competition. Harry's good looks have made him hugely popular around the globe and the band's US management are trying to make him into the lead singer, but despite the adoration, he does his best to stay grounded.

'I would never want to get bigheaded – it's such an unattractive trait and I can't imagine myself ever being like that. I always want to be aware of staying true to myself.'

Harry Styles

Louis

On Christmas Eve 1991, Louis William Tomlinson arrived, and since his parents split up when he was tiny, he took his stepfather Mark's surname. He has four younger stepsisters: Charlotte, Félicité and twins Daisy and Phoebe. As a child, he planned to become an actor and after finding himself an agent, he won small parts in the TV shows *Fat Friends*, *If I Had You* and *Waterloo Road*.

Louis attended acting school in Barnsley, South Yorkshire, but he was too busy having fun, filming and appearing in local plays, so ended up failing his first year of A-levels, following which he moved to a local comprehensive.

Louis first gained a reputation for being a prankster when he left *The X Factor* studios wearing a hospital gown. When the boys were on the *X Factor* Live Tour in February 2012, he landed himself in trouble for wrecking dressing rooms in Sheffield and Liverpool, where everyone was throwing fruit at the wall.

'Acting is something I would definitely think about pursuing later on, but for now it's all about the band.'

Louis Tomlinson

Here's Looking At You

Being catapulted from total obscurity into a world of superstardom where their every move is watched, discussed and analysed by armies of adoring fans has proved an overwhelming experience for Harry, Zayn, Liam, Niall and Louis. Although some moments are pretty hair-raising, especially when mobbed by huge crowds, the boys are slowly starting to get used to the glare of the spotlight. The first time they flew into Heathrow Airport together after *The X Factor*, they were stunned by the enormous throng of girls waiting for them.

'I want to sit on Harry Styles' lap!
I have a total crush on him.
He walked past me at the
Aquascutum show and I was
salivating; I like his curly hair
and he looks like a little cherub.'
It-girl Poppy Delevingne

'Every now and then you have like a
realization moment where you get
goosebumps and think: I am literally the
luckiest person in the world.'

Niall Horan

The Image

While millions of girls want to be with them, just as many boys want to look like One Direction and high streets everywhere are now full of copycat fashions. The first trend they sparked was quirky jumpsuits after they were spotted in *The X Factor* house wearing distinctive all-in-ones from Norwegian label OnePiece – Jump In. So many people wanted to get their hands on one that the Oslo-based designers sold out in days. It has also been good news for Toms, makers of the eco-friendly shoes that Louis always wears, and sales of the Fred Perry tennis trainers Niall prefers have also surged. After Harry was spotted in the front row of the Aquascutum catwalk show at London Fashion Week, the classic British label became cool all over again, in the process giving Harry a whole new set of fans.

We Love You

It should come as no great surprise that the boys have some very famous fans, including America's First Lady, Michelle Obama, who is so smitten that she invited them to the annual Easter Egg Hunt at the White House, held on Easter Monday 2012. Unfortunately, their hectic promotional schedule did not allow the visit, but they cheekily asked if they could come back another time. They have also caught the eye of Arnold Schwarzenegger's daughter Katherine, though Harry is perhaps understandably wary of the Terminator star!

'Imagine having Arnie as your dad-in-law!'

Harry Styles

The Directioners

Dedicated fans are known as 'Directioners' and they are so devoted to the boys' happiness that one girl from Boston was distraught when it rained in her hometown during the band's visit – in case it meant they would never come back! 'One Direction are in my city,' said Megan Connor, 'which means that I am breathing the same air as them.'

With girls permanently camped outside their homes and hotels, it seems they are living every teenage boy's dream; Harry admits that it can be a struggle not to let all the adoration go to their heads. 'We get a lot of praise,' he says. 'Obviously it's lovely to hear and it always puts a smile on your face but I want to keep my feet on the ground as much as possible.' British TV station Channel 4 is set to release a special documentary celebrating the Directioners die-hard devotion through social media in 2013. The one-off Cutting Edge special called *I Heart One Direction* aims to get under the skin of the most passionate fans to find out what it really means to be a Directioner.

'I really enjoyed performing and yet I never had the courage to do a whole school assembly because I was so intimidated. It's so weird to think that I've ended up performing in front of thousands!'

Louis Tomlinson

Here And Now

As they continue to top the charts and conquer hearts around the world, Harry, Liam, Zayn, Niall and Louis are busier than ever. Barely out of their teens, the boys have hectic daily schedules packed with sell-out concerts, TV performances and endless personal appearances. There is even a movie in the pipeline and they have taken America by storm, scooping three MTV Video Music Awards along the way.

Olympic Gold

The roar of the crowd was deafening as One Direction entered the Olympic Stadium on the back of a lorry to perform at the closing ceremony of London 2012. With a global audience of over one billion people, they knew the eyes of the entire world were on them as they played their biggest ever gig.

Take Me Home

In November 2012, a year after the UK release of *Up All Night*, the boys were thrilled to bring out *Take Me Home*, which went straight to No. 1 in over 35 countries, and sold over 1 million copies in its first week. They became the first boy band in US chart history to achieve two No. 1 albums in one calendar year. Released in September 2012, 'Live While You're Young' was the eagerly anticipated first single from the boys' new album, and, the song was a top 5 hit around the world. Their next single, 'Little Things', was released in the UK at the same time as the album, making the boys the first band to land a No. 1 in both the single and album charts at the same time.

The Tours

The shows for the first tour kicked off in Watford on 18 December 2011, ending in Belfast a month later. Then it was announced that there would be an Oceania leg of the tour, with dates across Australia and New Zealand set for April 2012, followed by 27 dates in America.

Before their 2012 tour was even over, the boys were already announcing plans for another one, which started in February 2013. Selling out in minutes, extra dates were added to an already gruelling schedule between February and October, making their 2013 World Tour a total of 117 shows in Europe, Australasia and North America.

In May 2013 the boys kept their army of fans on tenterhooks as their website ticked down to a mysterious announcement. Speculation was rife, with rumours that the band was unveiling a new member, a musical or even giving fans a chance to star in their movie. When the news finally broke that the boys would be embarking on another world tour in 2014, the site crashed due to the millions of Directioners desperate for details. The Where We Are Tour sees the boys taking to the biggest stadiums around the world, including Latin America and Europe. The tour is to support their new album, *Where We Are* (2013) which has 'a rockier and edgier tone to it'. It is predicted this will earn the boys a staggering £50 million between them.

'*My hopes for the future? To take over the world! You've got to aim high.*'

Louis Tomlinson

'As soon as we started recording music, we were aware that people would be surprised by it because it's not typical boy band music. There's nothing else out there like our sound at the moment, it's completely new – it's One Direction's sound and we love it!'

Zayn Malik

Charity Work

As ambassadors for the charity Rays of Sunshine, One Direction interrupted their world tour to pay a visit to cancer-stricken schoolgirl Niamh Power in May 2012. The eight-year-old was delighted at the surprise visit arranged through the charity, which grants wishes for seriously ill children. They also joined forces with JLS to record a single, a cover of Rose Royce's 'Wishing On A Star', for the children's charity Together For Short Lives, and in October 2011 Zayn posed topless to help raise funds for Teenage Cancer Trust.

In February 2013, One Direction released the hugely successful cover version of the iconic tracks 'One Way or Another' and 'Teenage Kicks' called 'One Way or Another (Teenage Kicks)'. It soared to the No. 1 position and as the 2013 Comic Relief single all proceeds went to the charity – now that's a lot of cash! The band performed the song at the 2013 BRIT Awards, where they also won the Global Success Award.

'This is our chance to have an amazing time, doing what we love to do and we're not going to let that pass us by for anything!'

Liam Payne

Making Movies…

Following on from the success of the boys' first DVD *Up All Night – The Live Tour* in May 2012, where they sent legions of fans into a frenzy by organizing a worldwide viewing party, the boys have upped the ante with their 2013 3D biopic film, *One Direction: This Is Us*, directed by Academy Award nominee Morgan Spurlock. The movie gives a rare glimpse of what the boys got up to behind the scenes on their recent tour. It also shows their families and features interviews with the boys describing their dreams and what their phenomenal rise to fame actually feels like. The poster for the documentary has caused a stir with its unique mosaic of thousands of fans, who were given the opportunity to send in their photos for publication.

The World At Their Feet

One Direction have defied even their fiercest critics and achieved what many assumed would be impossible: they have cracked not just America but Canada and Australia as well. They may be millionaires and in demand all over the world, but the boys are determined to keep their feet on the ground, no matter how famous they become. Although they have played in front of packed stadiums and Queen Elizabeth II, and appeared at the London 2012 Olympics Closing Ceremony and been immortalized as Madame Tussauds waxworks, the lads credit their tight-knit families and close friends with making sure they do not let the adoration go to their heads. Thanks to that, One Direction may well take over the world, and we can be sure they will do it with cheeky grins on their faces. We can't wait!

One Direction Vital Info

Niall

Birth Name:	Niall James Horan
Birth Date:	13 September 1993
Birth Place:	Mullingar, County Westmeath, Ireland
Height:	1.71 m (5 ft 7 in)
Star Sign:	Virgo

Harry

Birth Name:	Harry Edward Styles
Birth Date:	1 February 1994
Birth Place:	Holmes Chapel, Cheshire, England
Height:	1.77 m (5 ft 10 in)
Star Sign:	Aquarius

Liam

Birth Name:	Liam James Payne
Birth Date:	29 August 1993
Birth Place:	Wolverhampton, England
Height:	1.77 m (5 ft 10 in)
Star Sign:	Virgo

Louis

Birth Name:	Louis William Tomlinson
Birth Date:	24 December 1991
Birth Place:	Doncaster, South Yorkshire, England
Height:	1.75 m (5 ft 9 in)
Star Sign:	Capricorn

Zayn

Birth Name:	Zayn Javadd Malik
Birth Date:	12 January 1993
Birth Place:	Bradford, England
Height:	1.75 m (5 ft 9 in)
Star Sign:	Capricorn

Online

onedirectionmusic.com:	Official site in many languages, with news, photos, events and store
myspace.com/onedirection:	One Direction's latest songs and videos
facebook.com/onedirectionmusic:	Find out what 1D are up to
twitter.com/onedirection:	Share your thoughts with the 1D boys and other Directioners @onedirection
raysofsunshine.org.uk:	Charity granting wishes to seriously ill children aged 3–18
flametreepop.com:	Celebrity, fashion and pop news, with loads of links, downloads and free stuff!

Acknowledgements

Nadia Cohen (Author)
Nadia Cohen is an entertainment journalist who has worked at a number of national newspapers and magazines, including *Grazia* and the *Daily Mail*. As a showbusiness correspondent, she covered film festivals, premieres and award ceremonies around the world. Nadia was headhunted for the launch of a new American magazine, *In Touch Weekly*, and spent several years living and working in New York. Nadia now lives in London and juggles family life with showbiz news and gossip.

Mango Saul (Foreword)
Mango Saul has been a music, lifestyle and entertainment journalist for ten years. Some of his highlights include having breakfast at Waffle House with rapper Ludacris in Atlanta, sharing a bed with Destiny's Child for a *Smash Hits* cover interview and being sent an ice-cream costume for no reason. As editor of Sugarscape.com, Mango has seen the site grow to over 4 million page views per month and was shortlisted for Digital Editorial Individual 2011 at the AOP Awards.

Picture Credits
All images © **Getty Images**: FilmMagic: 1, 27, 28, 47; FOX Image Collection: 8; Getty Images Entertainment: 11, 12, 15, 16, 21, 24, front cover & 37, 41, 42; Getty Images for Jingle Ball 2012: 3 & 32 & back cover; Getty Images Sport: 7; WireImage: 18, 23, 31, 35, 38; WireImage for MuchMusic: 44.